# A Difficult Love

Collected Poems

Irma Kurti

**Ukiyoto Publishing**

All global publishing rights are held by

**Ukiyoto Publishing**

Published in 2024

Content Copyright © Irma Kurti

Cover Photo: Biagio Fortini

**ISBN 9789364947206**

*All rights reserved.*
*No part of this publication may be reproduced, transmitted, or stored in a retrieval system, in any form by any means, electronic, mechanical, photocopying, recording or otherwise, without the prior permission of the publisher.*

*The moral rights of the author have been asserted.*

*This is a work of fiction. Names, characters, businesses, places, events, locales, and incidents are either the products of the author's imagination or used in a fictitious manner. Any resemblance to actual persons, living or dead, or actual events is purely coincidental.*

*This book is sold subject to the condition that it shall not by way of trade or otherwise, be lent, resold, hired out or otherwise circulated, without the publisher's prior consent, in any form of binding or cover other than that in which it is published.*

www.ukiyoto.com

*To my parents, Hasan Kurti and Sherife Mezini,
to tell them that there is not a single day when I don't think
about them
and that they are inside me, in the safest place,
the soul, where only the greatest loves are preserved...*

# Preface

**IRMA KURTI**, Italian-Albanian poet and writer, with her beautiful and sincere verses that go straight to the reader's heart, answers the question of whether it is possible to write and poetize in a language other than one's mother tongue. This is a sensitive question, as also it encompasses the poetic attempt itself, but it is a successful endeavor in Kurti's case. Her writing, in its sincerity, is a pure, simple and beautiful poetry, so persuasive that it plucks the heartstrings with a certain "naivety"— just the kind that only children and poets possess.

In fact, while Kurti's collection, which consists of fifty poems on various themes and topics, appears smooth and easy, to poetize in another language is a Herculean effort that sometimes even borders on the Sisyphean. A difficult, poignant craft, underappreciated by many native speakers, writing in a second language is a valuable way to enrich both one's soul of origin and the "cultural" one that belongs to one through choice, destiny, life paths and who knows with what else.

Kurti's poetry travels poetically on two main tracks: on the first, it displays the theme of loneliness and, consequently, human alienation as seen through the poetic kaleidoscope of the poet's own lonely soul. The second poetic track of the collection, the most sensitive and the most touching one with which Kurti's entire opus is permeated, is the strand of a soul dripping with grief describing her great personal sadness and loss. In fact, the entire sylloge is dedicated to the memory of her parents, now her guardian angels, who departed for another dimension from which they yet inspire deep and unique tones and feelings; they are always watching over the poet's every lyrical step.

**Vesna Andrejević**

**Poet and literary critic**

# Contents

| | |
|---|---|
| The Radiography of My Life | 1 |
| I Want to Tell You | 3 |
| A Little Emotion | 5 |
| An Insecure Place | 6 |
| We Have Forgotten | 7 |
| The Sun Has Emigrated | 8 |
| The Testament | 9 |
| A Letter to Mom | 11 |
| Forgive Me! | 13 |
| The Doors of My Soul | 14 |
| On A Street with No Name | 15 |
| My Body and Soul | 17 |
| The Goodnight Kiss | 18 |
| We Decided to Cry | 19 |
| You Sleep | 20 |
| The Fires | 21 |
| The Christmas Fir Tree | 22 |
| It's Time to Love | 23 |
| A Cracked Soul | 24 |
| Leave This Sunset to Me | 26 |
| Looking Pain in The Eye | 27 |
| Lots of Shivers | 28 |
| On The Threshold of a Sorrow | 29 |
| This Spring | 31 |

| | |
|---|---|
| The Jacket of Sadness | 32 |
| An Unreal Memory | 33 |
| Usual | 35 |
| A Meeting with Mom | 36 |
| Unsatisfied | 37 |
| A Dusty Street | 38 |
| I See You So Clearly | 40 |
| Cell Phones | 41 |
| The Shadows of My City | 43 |
| A Thread of Grass | 45 |
| Where Do You Watch Me From? | 46 |
| His Bench Rests Empty | 47 |
| Winter Without You | 49 |
| A Candle in The Soul | 51 |
| Eternal Spring | 52 |
| Wounded Swallows | 53 |
| The Poppy | 54 |
| Late | 55 |
| What Was the World Like? | 56 |
| If Love Is This | 57 |
| Time To Say "Enough!" | 58 |
| Slaves | 59 |
| Angry With Life | 60 |
| We Won't Laugh Anymore | 62 |
| Open The Window! | 63 |
| A Difficult Love | 65 |

*About the Author* 67

# The Radiography of My Life

This is the radiography of my life and
there is nothing I can add, or take away.
In it, you find misty tears and pure joys—
who knows why you see so few words there.

The sounds and echoes that come from afar,
as from a dream that frightens in the night,
represent the voices of visions and illusions
that were shattered just like a piece of glass.

These stains scattered here and there that
resemble clouds tell of my long and silent
suffering, the evil and pains in that prison
that obliged me to leave my own country.

In an instant, I took my life into my hands
shouting: "I must definitely save myself!"
I emigrated, and a lot of my old wounds
have disappeared—others, perhaps remain.

Someone among you asked me a question,
asked if I feel healthy and healed now.
Well, for me, it's not easy to respond: "You
can never recover from nostalgia and love."

# I Want to Tell You

Today, I want to tell you my story,
picking up the shreds of my years.
It may sound slightly melancholic,
maybe it will even cause you tears.

But you have to be a bit sensitive
in order to shed a torrent of tears
in this chaotic world, where a lot
of people are soulless mannequins.

Today, I will tell you a happy story,
although it may not be such for you:
my bed is that green vast meadow,
I drink rain and get drunk too.

I am fascinated by the sea in winter,
by its strong and, at times, silent rage—
I fall in love with the wrinkles of the
elderly and a child's small footsteps.

I see that I have disillusioned you,
though I haven't told you all about
myself. I'd better leave you in your
world made of iPhones and Internet.

# A Little Emotion

I am looking for a little emotion,
as slight as the trembling of a leaf,
as slender as the swaying of grasses,
as gentle as the lapping of a wave at sea.

I'm not searching for a powerful
emotion that will shake me like
an earthquake, that will blind me
like a big illuminated mirror and
leave me sleepless in the night.

I am looking for a little emotion,
so that my heart can hold it up.

# An Insecure Place

The world has become an insecure
and fearful place at our every step.
We feel something, maybe anxiety,
in each journey, in every walk we take.

Dreams and games are interrupted,
loud shouts of innocent people are
heard, joys are veiled with anguish.
In a climate of terror, our days drip
raindrops of blood and so much sadness.

# We Have Forgotten

We have forgotten to take a walk
in a park, to sing a song without a
guitar, to watch the vibration of a
lake and the silent passage of ducks.

We have forgotten to lie down on the
grass admiring the sky, to caress an
animal for hours, to cry, not trying
to hide our limpid tears, but above
all: we have forgotten to exchange
a single word with someone that we love.

# The Sun Has Emigrated

To what lands has the sun emigrated?
It has left a monotonous gloomy sky,
and I see that I cannot find it here:
in my soul and in my thoughtful eyes.

Will it turn back to my country again?
It is warming other universes now.
There is fog, politics, so much chaos—
there are not any dreams and smiles.

Thousands of wrinkles tell stories of
people who try to leave and escape.
The buildings do not let one breathe—
luxury and hunger live together.

The sun has emigrated to other lands.

# The Testament

There is a season of life that I don't want
to live: the season of long, deep old age,
when memories abandon you one by one
and the body rests, like a rotten tree, inert.

A lot of those cold and unfeeling people
will come close to me, trying to help me.
There will be some who will make fun of
me and, behind my back, will laugh heartily.

Oh, they will lift me out of the wheelchair
like a mannequin is moved in the window,
and they will leave stains on my sluggish
body. Those will be imprinted in my soul.

I don't want to live that season of descent,
when no one listens to my heart's voice.
Please, throw me into the sea or leave me
in a forest where birds build their nests.

This is a testament: please open it when
my brain is like an empty glass.
I am writing fast, while I still can recall
and talk with memories of the distant past.

# A Letter to Mom

How are you, Mom? We haven't talked
for so long—I haven't received any news
from you, but there are signs that I decipher
like your tracks, like a greeting from you.

You promised me that you would come
and death would never separate us.
All my days have been transformed
into a waiting with quick beats of my heart.

Mother, I cannot come to you just now,
as hundreds of sleepy verses wait for me,
a lot of vague and confused ideas to be
changed on a sheet of paper into poetries.

Our memories often come to my mind:
our tiny kitchen and those dark nights,
the long evenings around a small stove
that were kindled by affection and love.

You knew how to keep your promises,
so I fear that something has happened.
I'll send a letter to you in your shelter,
cooled beneath the cypress tree shade.

# Forgive Me!

I could not be part of your happiness.
Forgive me. I watched you, listened
to you, so detached and numb. Those
sparks of your joy did not touch me,
and my smile was withered and dull.

As you told me about the chances of
your life made of shades and dazzling
colors, I felt deep in my chest just like
a knife, the pangs of my own anxieties.

# The Doors of My Soul

I decided not to know other people and
animals, thus to close my soul's doors,
because one day, I will surely lose them,
and then the wings of my joy will be cut off.

The few people that are part of my life
often give me thoughts and sadness,
anguish and numerous sleepless nights,
which for now, are just enough for me.

# On A Street with No Name

Today, on a street with no name,
surrounded by flowers and lots
of people, you suddenly came into
my mind and found a place there.

I never understood who I was in
your long chain of acquaintances
with no beginning, with no end.

You held my hand. I felt happy,
naïve, uncontrolled like a child;
the world was a unique, a better
place with the beauty of a poem.

Anger, sympathy, maybe nothing,
I don't know what I feel just now,
but I know that I found the address
of happiness without you, finally.

Today, on a street with no name,
surrounded by flowers and lots
of people, you suddenly came into
my mind and found a place there.

# My Body and Soul

My body is doing well in this period—
it walks and runs like an automaton,
and it collides with other robots in the
streets, with their elbows and arms.

There's no one that apologizes to you.
In the everydayness that's fed only on
technology, lots of words fade and die.

My body's doing well during this time—
my soul is broken into a thousand parts.

# The Goodnight Kiss

The goodnight kiss is a ritual now—
it lingers on my lips for a second,
but my sleep escapes, and I think
about that total absence of emotion.

I'll go down to the street and wait a
long time until the rains come and
kiss me passionately. In each drop,
I will lower my eyelids till the sun
is born within me. Then rains will
wash away the goodnight kiss.

# We Decided to Cry

The sky and I decided to cry
at the same time on the same
day. I don't know the reasons
for its tears, but I know mine
very well.

Someone is celebrating with
joy—this is just a usual day
for someone else. On this
day, many years ago, I lost
someone that I loved immensely.

The sky and I decided to cry.

# You Sleep

You rest peacefully immersed in a deep sleep:
neither the strongest winters can wake you now,
nor the rumble of thunder that comes as a grunt,
nor the sounds of this obscure and desolate sky.

Not even this feeling that pulses in my heart
for you, my voice that is changed into a scream,
not even the echo of all our shared memories,
the chirping of the birds, that sweet symphony.

Not even the rivers of my tears wake you up,
so I have to swallow my shout like bread;
it crashes into the abyss found within me,
and then it suddenly vanishes to be born again.

Yet your smile is without a shadow of sadness,
just as you had it in your life: serene, calm.
That alone confuses me, so I don't know what
to do: wake you up or just let you sleep, Mom?

# The Fires

It is nothing else, only a bit of nostalgia
in this foggy, cold and anonymous city,
where all the days are the same, where
a pure and a limpid soul is broken.

It is nothing else, just a memory that this
winter brought me from afar—the image
of an old stove and our frozen hands on it.
My dear mother blew on a fire that didn't
light at all. Sparks were flying in the room
like a thousand shining stars.

Her breath lit the embers and, in the soul,
the fire of love and affection. Now that
she is not here anymore, all the fires are
extinguished. Maybe forever.

# The Christmas Fir Tree

You will no longer come for Christmas,
and I see thousands of lights in the street
fading away slowly.

The fir tree begins to wither in my soul,
and leaves are falling now. I feel naked
and so fragile!

You will no longer come for Christmas,
and you won't open your presents. My
heart will rest locked forever.

The Christmas fir tree is losing leaves
in the depths of my soul continuously.

# It's Time to Love

It is time to love each other,
even a little bit; let rancor and
hatred melt like avalanches.
They will become powerful
rivers that flow toward seas.

Let's draw on our faces wide
smiles, warm as the rays of the
sun. Words and prejudices will
vanish and our embraces will
become even bigger. Within,
there will be room for all of us.

It is time to love…

# A Cracked Soul

The days watched us as we wore
rubber sandals and black aprons.
We were two little girls, but your
insults in my ears are still echoing.

How much cynicism, how many
words undressed of every particle
of friendship and love! They often
wounded me more than guns, and
on my slender body they left scars.

I have tried to consign to oblivion
you and the episodes of my remote
past, but who knows why the hands
of time stop on that memory now.

Don't be surprised if I cannot open
to you the doors of friendship today
and tomorrow; there are words one

cannot bury, and the soul remains
cracked and forever broken.

# Leave This Sunset to Me

Leave this sunset to me, the clouds red
as if they feel guilty; I am sure, the most
talented painter would not succeed in
immortalizing on his canvas such beauty.

This time I won't compare the sun to a
big ball of fire but to a shining eye in
love, which is trying to enter so gently
inside its lowered eyelids.

I will stay true to its charm, its mixed
colors of the rainbow, to the chills that
run through my body and soul, just like
fingers on the piano keyboard.

Leave this sunset to me.

# Looking Pain in The Eye

It is time to look pain in the eye,
make it an integral part of my life,
allow the tears to dry on my cheeks,
swallow sighs and moans in silence.

How many times did I hide myself so
as to avoid it? I wasted endless months
and years. I ran, but the pain was faster,
and with its claws, it was able to catch
me. It is time to look pain in the eye.

# Lots of Shivers

There is a deep peace in the morning,
which has heard only the sound of my
heels, but it fades slowly like the slight
rustle of wings.

An imperceptible breeze blows, and
lots of shivers run through the leaves;
the remote and timid rays of the sun
now play hide-and-seek with the trees.

# On The Threshold of a Sorrow

I would like to enter your great sorrow
as though entering a well that is dark,
share with you tears and anxieties, listen
to the thin, trembling voice of your heart.

I have often entered the suffering spirit of
my friends and have cried for them like a
child. Sometimes my days were so gray,
it seemed to me that this life wasn't mine.

The indifference of people has struck my
body and soul like a whip; the anguish
has taken refuge in my wound. It is still
there, and it never wants to leave me.

Today, maybe only today, I prefer to stay
on the threshold of your sorrow so as not
to be carried away by rivers of tears into

the abyss without any lights or glow.

I'll stay on the threshold of your sorrow…

# This Spring

I want to enjoy this spring,
contemplate the blue sky,
lie down casually on the
grass and get drunk with
myriad scents and colors.

I want to open the windows
of my soul and let the wind
caress it, smell the flowers
and awaken under a rainbow.

I want to enjoy this spring
and let the pain melt like snow.

# The Jacket of Sadness

Under the faint neon light, shadows of people pass by. It's raining, and the street is sleepy and deserted, while the wind refuses to bring me a message from you now.

I keep waiting for you with an imperceptible anguish, just as spring awaits the return of a migratory bird from a long journey.

Time drags on. The air clings to me with a sense of emptiness; the roads seem abandoned, and my soul is a mixture of rain and tears.

My heart keeps calling you, but you do not answer. I stand still. Life is also this instant: waiting for you restively, on my shoulders, a jacket of sadness.

# An Unreal Memory

You walk away at a slow pace on the road;
the wind is playing with your hair now.
I used to go crazy for that hair. I watch you,
just as someone might watch a passerby.

I ran my fingers so often through your hair.
It was your embrace that saved me from the
world. We both dreamed of an eternal love,
but ours was only a fragment, an episode.

I believed I had touched the magic of love,
and that we would walk together forever,
but now I feel like I didn't know you at all.
Oh, our journey was so short!

And I can no longer shout, "Please, stay!"
I watch you until you become a little stain,
remorse and nostalgia are mixed within me,
then, like an unreal memory, you fade away.

You walk away at a slow pace on the road;
the wind is playing with your hair now.
I used to go crazy for that hair. I watch you,
just as someone might watch a passerby.

# Usual

It has become so usual to insult one another with arrogance and swear words, venting anger like poison, sowing hatred and also suffocating the peace.

It has become so usual that our soul doesn't open itself like a flower within a great hug, and we are changed into mean people, little by little, abandoning calmness and silence.

It has become so usual with relatives to cross paths and not exchange a single word, feeling that the same blood flowing in our veins does not unite us but instead drives us apart.

It has become so usual that innocent people are being killed every day. But love, that is unusual: it has thus become a memory, a relic in a museum.

# A Meeting with Mom

I was knocking on the door of my house,
but no one opened it. That was strange!
My fingers were hurting so much, and I
was feeling exhausted and stressed.

Suddenly, I heard my mom's voice saying,
"My daughter, I didn't expect you now."
I didn't understand why she was cold and
aloof. I was not part of her love anymore.

She opened the doors of the world to me
with her warm, unique, immense hug.
A tear just like a pearl quickly fell down
on the threshold of my childhood house.

It was only a dream. I felt lonely and sad
that the meeting with my mom was short.
Even if she didn't open the door to me, it
would be enough to hear her sweet voice!

# Unsatisfied

We are unsatisfied when it is sunny
and when it rains and the weather is
obscure and gloomy. In the winter,
we look for the spring, but when it
is very hot, we dream of coldness.

There's nothing that pleases us and
nothing makes us happy; there'll
always be something wrong. We don't
see that time passes, flies by, mocking
the frustration and discontent of us all.

# A Dusty Street

The two of us don't live
far apart: a dusty street
divides us. I often pass
that way; the horns and
noises cover the cries
of memories of our past.

I fear your cold glance.
Your cynicism knows no
end! You weigh my every
word. You are young, but
in your soul rules only
darkness and resentment.

I don't know if one day
you'll love me with the
purity of the past. Will
you see that nothing has
happened, that blood is

thicker than water? Will
you free yourself from
anger and resentment?

I've often asked myself:
"What divides love from
hatred? The thin paper
of a cigar, a fragile
and delicate thread?"

Life is being shortened
mercilessly with the giant
scissors of a dressmaker,
chasms deepen, loves fade
away. You and me remain
separated by a dusty street.

# I See You So Clearly

Sometimes, your portrait is so vivid,
with that soft look, with your smile,
with your hug that fades away my fears.

I see you in front of me so clearly,
regardless of whether it's foggy out
there, whether it's regularly raining
or there is no sun here.

Your presence is clear just like you;
it surpasses the thought that you aren't
anymore among us. Life finds its colors
at once.

I see you so clearly that it seems strange
that I cannot embrace you, that I cannot
talk to you endlessly.

Dad!

# Cell Phones

I called my mom; the cell phone
that evening was always ringing,
but she did not answer. Anguish
and concern slowly invaded me.

How could you not hear that call,
how could it not reach you, Mom?
You used to hear my every sigh,
my every moan in the deep night.

You distinguished immediately
every single teardrop in my eyes.
You could feel the quick beats of
my sad, weary, hopeless heart.

It was a dream again! Suddenly,
grief covered me like a veil.
My mother can no longer return
and my affliction grew stronger.

I'd have thrown away all the cell
phones into a pond, a sea or lake,
to be near you, my beloved mom,
for a single moment once again!

# The Shadows of My City

You come in groups to visit this city
and stop in every inch of it; you take
lots of photos, admiring it in silence.

You come in groups to visit this city,
where the churches shiver in the brash
sounds of the bells. You try to grasp
the few rays of sun that the high
buildings often take hostage.

You are surprised by the sculptures
erected on the square that stare at
you like mute witnesses. A bit
farther, the fashion stores with
high prices invite you to enter.

But you do not know: in the night
and in the dark, my city is invaded
by those persons - silhouettes that

sigh. They don't have roofs over
their heads. They are the ones who
don't freeze from the harsh climate
but from lack of love.

Those are the shadows… of my city.

# A Thread of Grass

I keep thinking about you on
this trip, and I feel how a lot
of memories knock at my soul.
We planned to travel together,
but life separates people, death
even more so. I am surrounded
by people who enjoy autumn,
and I feel the wind touching my
hair. I see the leaves dance, but
I remain only a stranger to it all.

I try to understand the meaning
of a sunny day without you. So
I wander in those places where
you walked, and a blade of grass
tries in a hurry, before it is
trampled by children, to tell
me something new or maybe to
convey a message that you left
before you went away forever.

# Where Do You Watch Me From?

What point of the sky are you looking from,
from which flower or leaf, from which palm
tree, from what blue-colored swimming pool?
From a red rose or from a magnolia that
scatters fragrance everywhere, from where
does your anima watch me?

I stay here and wait for a single signal from
you, to hear a sound, maybe just your voice.
I lie down on the bed, turning around again
and again, but I find no calm in the hotel
where you slept.

What point of the sky are you looking from,
from which flower or leaf, from which palm
tree, from what blue-colored swimming pool?
From where, my beloved father, does your
anima watch me?

# His Bench Rests Empty

Surely, you must have seen a man
passing here in the morning, with
slow steps walking by, caressing
the flowers with his look, before he
would sit on that bench over there.

Surely, you must have seen a man
with a bright smile like a ray
of sun—he was so kind and full of
goodness. He waved his head
slightly; he spoke little but listened
so much.

But none of you has ever asked
why he doesn't walk here anymore,
the echo of his footsteps cannot
be heard, and his bench rests empty—
covered with leaves it waits still.

That meek and gentle person of
few words that you met by chance;
that was my beloved father…

# Winter Without You

The first winter without you.
Behind the windowpane, now
I look at the emptiness that is
stretching out in front of me,
and my breath draws slowly
on its surface stains of
melancholy.

I feel you close as you stare
like a child at the white
snow. I listen to your voice,
as sweet as music, that
whispers to me: "It is cold,
and I won't go out. I'll stay
here with you…"

The steam of the coffee
we sipped in the evenings
together always protected

me from storms and rain.

The blanket of snow does
not extend only to the streets
but inside my house too.
I stray in the vortex of this
infinite winter without you.

# A Candle in The Soul

There is a candle burning in my soul;
it produces nostalgia and affliction. It
burns endlessly whether there's sunshine
or rain. The wind, the storms, my limpid
incessant tears can never extinguish its
flame. It will be snuffed only when I
close my eyes and take my last breath.

# Eternal Spring

Parents, I want to imagine you so happy
walking slowly and holding hands,
sitting in a green park, talking, dreaming
of us, your daughters, sharing your love.

I want to imagine you following us with
your eyes just as you did once, with that
goodness you passed on to us, while
we struggle to mask that abyss that your
journey with no return has left among us.

I want to imagine you tranquil in a world
full of light and serenity, where there is no
pain and suffering, no sickness and poverty,
where there is only one season: eternal spring.

# Wounded Swallows

You rise like an automaton long before dawn,
and in that silence the closing of a door is heard;
your footsteps resemble those of a drunkard.
A bit of bread is wrapped in a piece of paper.

It is a long way by train and by bus. The hours
drag on, and the sun does not yet rise; people are
gloomy, resembling the cloudy sky. They close
their mouths and don't pronounce a single word.

Evening comes, and you return to your warm nest
where your loves await you; you are so tired
that you cannot smile, and your head hangs over
the couch. Early in the morning, you set the
alarm clock again. In your chest, dreams vanish
and twist like wounded swallows that fall to
the ground.

# The Poppy

I did not plant this poppy for you
in your last abode, my dear Dad—
no hand would have planted it so
well next to the thin grass blades.

I did not plant this poppy for you;
I only know that you loved it so
much in your life. Now, I stand in
silence in front of it, thoughtful
and a bit dazzled too.

Maybe the spring that you adored,
the nature that has now engulfed
you as part of itself, has grown it
to flourish, to let us talk, through
its fragile petals, together.

# Late

You come late to dinner when my body
draws along a dull and monotonous day,
when it slowly dies, when my every cell
is tired, when the minutes and the hours
crumble in my fingers like grains of sand.

You come back late when I do not have
any desire to make you happy, when I've
shared all my sorrows with others, even
more with myself, when I think that one
day, like a flower, our love will blossom.

You come back late and don't understand
that now I am in love with the loneliness.

# What Was the World Like?

What was the world like when I was born: savage, unfair, cruel? Were there cold and indifferent people? Did they put on masks as they do today, so as to protect others from the virus of hypocrisy?

How was the world—was there wickedness in the soul, false smiles, traps behind your back? Mom, I don't want to ask you many questions, and I don't want to tire you out. I want to know: "How did you cope with the attacks, did they leave you sleepless? Did you sometimes want to lock yourself up with a big key in a cave to never leave again? Please, answer me, dear Mom!

# If Love Is This

What is this impetuous flow of people
who rush today only to shake my hand,
showering me with phrases of affection,
suffocating me, not letting me breathe?

Where were they hiding in those years
when I needed only a word, when I was
immersed in lethargic sleep with the
blanket of loneliness wrapped around me?

Where were they hiding in those days
when I dreamed of a bit of light, when
verses were huddled in a corner, and an
affectionate embrace would have opened
to me all the doors of the world?

And now, what am I supposed to do
with this *love*, if love it can be called?

# Time To Say "Enough!"

The others seek forgiveness from you.
What does it cost you? You have given
it before. Throw an insult, rancor,
like pebbles at the bottom of a void.

They forget your nights full of anguish,
your soul that complains; not even you
know that the words of the past haven't
vanished but make you suffer even more.

They forget that sadness and despair often
break your heart and you can't even breathe
deeply. You search in vain for a refuge, and
a little bit of serenity and calm.

In the end, you still forgive them; you
don't see that time has come to pronounce
"Enough!", to abandon the fake peace,
to fall in love with the walls of your house.

# Slaves

We have become slaves of technology:
in our hands, we clutch cell phones or
iPads; we've forgotten to open our stiff
lips as the train continues its long trip.

We don't see beyond the window how
nature extends its green arms, the storms
of birds flying toward foreign lands,
or the sleepy sky before sunrise.

If someone asks us a question, we all
stutter—we have forgotten how to talk.
Our fingers are on the cell phone as on
a piano. Its deaf sounds pull us away
from the beauties of everyday life.

# Angry With Life

I have often been angry with life.
Its slap remained on my face
when I knew the wrong people
who mocked my sentiments of love.

Life seemed vile to me in the days
when I was quiet, relaxed or happy;
it robbed me of even the joy of living
when it gave me great pains.

I often stumbled and hurt myself
in the invisible traps on the roads.
I hated life in my solitude: I asked
questions, but it did not reply at all.

I found my smile amidst my tears;
I started to worship it like a work
of art. My afflictions and troubles
lessened, and I was enchanted by

rare beauty and the magic of life.

My anger vanished like a cloud.

# We Won't Laugh Anymore

We won't laugh anymore as we used to:
happy, casual, carefree, with a dreamy
look and crystal-clear sounds, with that
feeling of being protected from all evil.

We won't laugh anymore as we used to:
with the thought that joy and happiness
have no end and neither does life, that
love may be found everywhere—in a
bud that opens, in the beating of a
bird's wings, on a sunny, rainy or cloudy
day, in a shell that waits for a kiss from
the waves.

We won't laugh anymore as we did then—
at the time, we were only innocent children.

# Open The Window!

Open the window—you can't live
in the dark! Let the air permeate
to every edge. The light with its
reflections, the sounds, the joys
and the emotions will also enter.

Do you think I haven't suffered
and my soul has not shed tears?
A single day, a week would not
be enough to tell you. Nobody
understood me any time I got
hurt and cried. It was like in a
movie: I didn't have a voice to shout.

There were some days, months,
years that I was feeling lonelier
than solitude itself, but now, all
has faded like a dense fog and
sun rays kiss me every morning.

Open the window…

# A Difficult Love

My love for this remote and distant city
is so strong, it fills my chest like oxygen.
It often takes away my desire to visit it,
transforming the desire into resentment.

The sad memories wake from delirium
and like moths begin to gnaw at my spirit,
fill my life with poison as in the past,
the slag heaps and gossips filled the air.

My childish world, as sheer as crystal,
cracked at the gossips and the ignorance.
I regret the years that in the calendar of
my heart haven't left the slightest trace.

Time passes, the city draws me like a
magnet. Lots of voices like scattered
musical notes shake me. I look at myself
with long hair gathered in a tail as I sing

happily and full of emotion on a stage.

The immense park of that city where my parents and I used to walk, glad and calm, appears in my dreams. I imagine heaven like this, with toys scattered on the grass.

My hatred and resentment subside until I no longer feel them. I want to visit my city's soil for a single instant, to kneel down, kiss, hold tightly between my fingers a piece of land that my parents trampled each day.

# About the Author

**Irma Kurti**

**IRMA KURTI** is an Albanian poet, writer, lyricist, journalist, and translator and has been writing since she was a child. She is a naturalized Italian and lives in Bergamo, Italy. All her books are dedicated to the memory of her beloved parents, Hasan Kurti and Sherife Mezini, who have supported and encouraged every step of her literary path.

Kurti has won numerous literary prizes and awards in Albania, Italy, Switzerland, USA, Philippines, Lebanon and China. She was awarded the Universum Donna International Prize IX Edition 2013 for Literature and received a lifetime nomination as an Ambassador of Peace by the University of Peace, Italian Switzerland. In 2020, she became the honorary president of WikiPoesia, the encyclopedia of poetry.

In 2022, she was nominated as the Albanian ambassador to the International Academic Award of Contemporary Literature Seneca of the Academy of Philosophical Arts and Sciences, Bari.

That same year, she was awarded the title of Mother Foundress and Lady of the Order of Dante Alighieri by the Republic of Poets.

She received the Grazia Deledda medal and diploma of merit from the National Committee of WikiPoesia on the 150th anniversary of the birth of the great Italian poet.

In 2023 she was awarded a Career Award from the Universum Academy Switzerland. She also won the prestigious 2023 Naji Naaman's literary prize for complete work.

Irma Kurti is a member of the jury for several literary competitions in Italy. She is also a translator for the Ithaca Foundation in Spain.

Irma Kurti has published 29 books in Albanian, 25 in Italian, 15 in English, and two in French. She has also translated 20 books by different authors, and all of her own books into Italian and English.

Irma Kurti is one of the most translated and published Albanian poets. Her books have been translated and published in the United States, Canada, France, Italy, Greece, Belgium, Netherlands, Romania, Turkey, Kosovo, the Philippines, Cameroon, India, Chile, Serbia and Colombia.

www.ingramcontent.com/pod-product-compliance
Lightning Source LLC
LaVergne TN
LVHW041543070526
838199LV00046B/1809